THE WORLD OF YESTERDAY

EVERY DAY IS A NEW ONE

SUNDARAM DUBEY

Its dedicated to INDIA of the past and now the present, there have been many changes and we have also adopted them. there ups and downs between past vs present. Past was better as compared to health of the present and the futture, but present is better from past in the way of cure of pandemics

Contents

1. India In The Past   1

2. The Fake Developers (british) Of India Says,   3

3. Difference In The Past And Present Life   11

4. Live With The Present As India Does   15

CHAPTER I

INDIA in the past

We Indians are great minded, int the past we were the most prosperous and very rich in our own independent economy. There were kings who were very liberal, and a sudden hit!.

The foriegns discovered INDIA for the first time ever, there were the french the protugese and the british (worstest of the all). they wer from yhe west and were new to the east. The french and protugese were not an issue. We indians are so big hearted that we accepted them gave them place in our own land, but who knewd that this was our biggest mistake.

By the time they discovered us we had already devolped a lot, like the vedic math, vedas and their records, our own way of reasearch in science, natural medicines the only mistake was to let the intuders see our treasure. The uk or the ehole england takne togethere would have not been much famous or rich in thier wealth. UK (british) had looted 18 trillion dollars. At that time our 1 one rupee was at the cost of 2 dollars (in america).

The problem was not with the invaders, the problem was with us. We INDIANS think by our heart not by our mind. they stole huge wealth at first but we forgave them as they wealth they looted the first time we let them in was huge for them but not for us. Theres an old saying of the INDIAN culture and tradition; "The guestes should be treated as gods".

they said we want food and we gave them, they said we want to go home but not empty hand so we handed them our special spices that was not in the west. Infact this so called fake devolpers of India had never seen our heard os spices, muslin cloths and many other fibres, not event their illitratde ancestors who were the tribal people. The best example was the blue revolution, the rich blue colou-INDIGO would have not been in their hands. At last they said we want land and indeed we gave them(the biggest mistakes of INDIA of all time)

they got everything they eanted, they thought they were clever to fool INDIANS ny their dirty biusness tricks of bying in low and sellin the same in high.But we the INDIANS respectd our past, our culture and acted as if we dont konw or we dont care. they started to flourish the goods, brought many workers formed an troop attacked the ruler of west bengal, captured, killed, bribed his assistans and continuedd this same ugly trick to cover whole of India.

And this sons of the f##king bi#ches said tht they were devolping INDIA, huh?. But we knew the reality and still didnt give them a damn f##k about thir misdeeds. when we thought its the time we finally revolted in late 80's.

CHAPTER II

The fake developers (British) of India says,

The period 1700 to 1900 saw the beginnings, and the development, of the British Empire in India. Empire was not planned, at least not in the early stages. In a sense, it just happened. The first British in India came for trade, not territory; they were businessmen, not conquerors. It can be argued that they came from a culture that was inferior, and a political entity that was weaker, than that into which they ventured, and they came hat-in-hand. They would not have been viewed as a threat by the Indians—who most certainly would not have thought of themselves as "Indian," at least in any political sense. National identity was to be established much later, during the Independence Movement (which, indeed, was also known as the Nationalist Movement). Identity was in terms of region and caste, which, to a considerable extent, it still is today. The British and the Indians would go on to affect each other in profound ways that still are important today. In what follows, because of limited space, the impact of Imperial Britain on India is addressed. Hopefully, a future useful essay on the impact of India on Great Britain will also be published in EAA.

The Roots of Empire

While there is no 1492-type date for the commencement of empire, 1757, the date of the Battle of Plassey, is often used. The date of the British take-over of Delhi, 1803, is symbolic: the British occupied the Mughul capital and were not to leave. The empire was neither uniform—different policies responding to different events in different parts of India—nor static. It was upon the British and the Indians almost before they realized it. Its effects were ambiguous and ambivalent. A recent catalog advertising DVDs said about a presentation entitled "The British Empire in Color,"

The British Empire brought education, technology, law and democracy to the four corners of the globe. It also brought prejudice, discrimination, cultural bigotry and racism.

The blurb goes on to state that the video "examines the complexities, contradictions, and legacies of empire, both positive and negative."1 To a degree, such is the intent of this article. Only to a degree, for an article this brief on a topic as complex and intricate as the British impact on India cannot be complete and faces the danger of becoming simply an inventory.

Trade and Power

In 1600, a group of English merchants secured a royal charter for purposes of trading in the East Indies. The Dutch, however, had fairly well sealed off trade in what is now Indonesia, and the merchants' company, which was to become known as the East India Company (the Company), turned its attention to the vast expanse of India, with its cotton and spices (e.g., "pepper" and "ginger" are from south Indian words), as well as other commodities. Other powers, especially the French and Portuguese, were to become competitors. The Portuguese secured enclaves on the west coast, the most important of which was Goa, which they controlled until 1961, and which preserves a Portuguese flavor to this day. The French secured influence in the southeast, where Puducherry, formerly Pondicherry, is sometimes referred to as "The French Riviera of the East," and was transferred to Indian jurisdiction in 1954.

The dominant power in India was the Mughal Empire. British adventurers had preceded the Company into India, including at the Mughal court. It needs to be emphasized that the purpose of the Company was trade. But a combination of factors and events were to draw the Company into Indian politics, especially with the decline of the Mughal Empire and the concurrent and resulting rise of regional powers, including that of the British, who had become ensconced at what is now Chennai (Madras), Mumbai (Bombay), and Kolkata (Calcutta).2 It is noteworthy that these three cities were founded (or at least developed) by the British, and in recent years have each had their names de-Anglicized.

Mughal Decline

Two events, fifty years apart, had important consequences. The first was the death in 1707 of the last of the "Great Mughals," Aurangzeb, who was followed by "lesser Mughals."3 In various ways, Aurangzeb's own policies may have contributed significantly to the Mughal decline, but the importance of his demise is that it was followed by incapable successors and considerable instability.

The British took advantage of the instability and the resulting regional tensions, especially in 1757 at the Battle of Plassey in Bengal. Through machinations and intrigues, a force of eight hundred Europeans and 2,200 Indian troops under Robert Clive defeated an army of 50,000 belonging to the ruler of Bengal. Clive was able to wrest concessions from the Mughals, most importantly the right of land revenue, and, in retrospect, it appears that an empire was underway.

Other challenges arose for the Mughals, including the rise of regional and ethnic powers such as the Marathas, Sikhs, and Rajputs, and the sack of Delhi in 1739 by the Persian invader Nadir Shah. Meanwhile, the British were to win out in south India over the French, largely because of the Anglo-French wars in Europe and North America in the 1740s.

The Company

The Company's increase in power and territory did not go unnoticed in London. In 1792, the Company applied for a loan from the government, which Parliament provided, but with strings attached: The Regulating Act of 1793, the first of a series of acts reining in the Company through parliamentary supervision. Nevertheless, Arthur Wellesley, as governor-general (1797–1805), exercised his intention to make the Company the paramount power in India. He was able to suppress what French influence remained (except for some small enclaves, such as Pondicherry), and to remove powerful Indian forces in both the north and the south. The British (that is the Company; in India the two were now to be almost synonymous until 1858) were paramount, and they developed a bureaucratic infrastructure, employing cooperating Indians, who came to constitute a new, urban class.

The title of Governor-General had been bestowed upon the governor of the Bengal presidency (Calcutta), who had been granted power and rank over the governors of the Bombay and Madras presidencies. This arrangement, provided in the Regulating Act, was felt to be necessary because of the long distance between London and India (the Suez canal did not yet exist) and the convenience of dealing with one governor rather than three: an administrative step toward unity which certainly aided the arrangement for empire.

The series of acts passed by Parliament banned private trading on the part of Company employees and separated judicial and administrative functions of the Company from commercial ones. The attempt was to regulate taxation, justice, rule, and bribery (the last being viewed by Company servants as an indispensable feature of doing business in India). The Company had acquired considerable political power (although consisting of only a fraction of one percent of the population of the subcontinent), over more people than there were in England. Parliament was concerned, and was to remain so. Empire may not have been, at this early stage, a governmental declaration, but the wheels were in motion and Parliament became a core part of it all. The India Act of 1784 created a council of six commissioners, including the Chancellor of the Exchequer and a newly-created Secretary of State for India. This group was constituted above the Company directors in London.

With the transition of the Company to the role of ruler, the British attitude toward Indians degenerated. Previously, there had been some limited social mixing between the British and Indians, with no sense of superiority or inferiority. That changed. What earlier Englishmen had viewed with interest in Indian culture became abomination; thus, the parliamentary leader against the slave trade, William Wilberforce (1759–1833) felt Hinduism to be a greater evil than slavery. The opening of the Suez Canal (1869) allowed greater access to India by English women—who, of course, had to be "protected" from the hostile culture and barbarous Indian men. Biased concepts regarding non-Western cultures and non-white peoples, arising from so-called social Darwinism and evangelicalism, provided rationale for imperial rule. It is not coincidence that the heyday of imperialism was the Victorian age.

Although the foundation was provided by the Battle of Plassey (1757), 1803 is a good symbolic date for the start of empire. General Gerard Lake defeated the Marathas, perhaps the most important Indian power, and entered Delhi, the Mughal capital. By this time the emperor was mostly a figurehead, but symbolically important. He now became a pensioner of the British, with his realm reduced to the Red Fort. A British official, referred to as the Resident, became de facto ruler of Delhi. Company soldiers protected the city and commercial interests. Things were never to be the same. In a sense, the taking of Delhi was but part of a process, for, as Dilip Hiro, in his chronology of Indian history has asserted, "By the late 18th century it had become commonplace among the British, irrespective of class, to despise Indians." This characterization has been affirmed by other observers.4

Racism and Rebellion

Racism is a core characteristic of the British Empire in India, or, as it came to be known, the Raj (from a Sanskrit word, which found its way into vernacular languages, meaning to rule over, or the sovereign who does so). Historically, the term was applied to Hindu kings (as raja, or maharaja, great king). While implying political superiority, it did not have racial implications. Cultural and political factors were to add racial distinction to the concept under the British: Christian proselytizing and the great uprising, or rebellion, or mutiny, of 1857. This historic rebellion was not an insurrection, for it was not organized, and therein may have been its failure.5

The rebellion was a bloody mess, involving Indian soldiers (sepoys), native rulers of "subsidiary" or "princely" states that were quasi-independent but in thrall to the Company (and in fear of loss of their principalities), and the Company armies, in vicious retaliation. In essence, it was an explosion of deep frustration and fear that had been building up for decades. It is significant that it was largely confined to north central India, where Company rule and British oppression were strongest and most obvious.

The causes were numerous, and included forcing the use of Western technologies—the railroad and telegraph—upon a highly traditional society, imposition of English as the language for courts and government schools, opening the country to missionaries (with the resulting fear of forced conversions), Company takeover of subsidiary states when a prince died without direct heir, increasing haughtiness and distance on the part of the rulers, and policies beneficial to the Company's profits, but even inimical to the people, and so on. The spark was the introduction of the Enfield rifle to the sepoy ranks, which necessitated handling of cartridges packed in animal grease, anathema for both Hindus and Muslims, and considered as an attempt to Christianize the sepoys. Atrocities became commonplace on both sides, and were to be repeated by the British in the Amritsar Massacre of 1919.

The rebellion and the gruesome reaction to it were atrocious enough, but, as Maria Misra has observed, "The after-shock of the Rebellion was if anything even more influential than the event itself."6 A curtain had fallen, and the two sides would never trust each other again. British disdain increased, and for the Indians, resentment festered. Yet oddly enough, Western influence was eclectically accepted by many upper class urban Indians (to a large extent in imitation, but also as a means to, and result of, upward mobility). The apparent anomaly of interest in things Western is best illustrated by Calcutta, one of the three early centers of Company presence. The others were Madras and Bombay— cities that built up around the Company's commercial establishment.

Indian Culture

Bengal historically has been marked by cultural pride, most justly so. Its position in Indian culture has been compared with that of Italy in European culture. Given different historical situations, the comparison might have gone the other way. Western impact was central to Calcutta (particularly noticeable in its architecture), the capital of British India, and provided the impetus for what is known as the Bengal Renaissance. As in Florence, it was business that made revival of the arts possible. In the case of Bengal, the revival involved religion as well. An almost perfect paradigm is that of the Tagore family. The modern founder was Dwarkanath Tagore (1794–1846), an entrepreneur with British partners and British friends, including women. His association with the relative freedom of English women, in contrast to the rigidly orthodox outlook of the women in his household, resulted in part with his becoming "a strong advocate of female education."7 The fortune he accumulated enabled his heirs to pursue other interests.

Dwarkanath's son Debendranath (1817–1905) was active in social and religious reform, especially the revitalization of Hinduism, largely in response to missionary activity resulting in conversions of Hindus to Christianity. He was also active in the 1850s in forming the British Indian Association, a forerunner of the Indian National Congress.

Debendranath was father of the famed Rabindranath (1861– 1941), an artistic genius and winner of the Nobel Prize for Literature in 1913. Several other Tagores were active in the arts and influential in the revitalization of Bengali culture.

A fascinating example of this revitalization is a style of painting dating from about 1800. Kalighat painting originated around a temple dedicated to the goddess Kali in a neighborhood near the Hooghly River. The subject matter was in part religious, but in a sensual manner, and it also focused on daily life. A favorite topic was the babu, who in this context was a quasi-Westernized dandy obsessed with shady women. (The term babu has many connotations.) As a form, the art anticipated some Western developments, but received little recognition from Westerners, the general attitude being reflected by John Ruskin's dismissal of all Indian art as that of "heathen people." Missionaries showed a negative interest, viewing the paintings as childish and evil at the same time. The art was an urban twist upon folk tradition, yet with its own freshness and uniqueness.

After 1857

There were decisive changes as a result of 1857. The Mughal dynasty was terminated, as was the Company. The British government took over direct rule, replacing the Company's administrative apparatus with an Indian Civil Service (which became the Indian Administrative Service after independence). In 1877, Queen Victoria was proclaimed Empress of India, a symbolic exclamation point.

Governor-Generals, popularly referred to as Viceroys (after 1858), came and went, but the direction remained clear: Imperial rule for the profit of Britain, not for the welfare of the people of India—this was shown even in the governmental response to famines, and India became represented as the Jewel in the Crown. With the formation of the Indian National Congress (or, simply, Congress), some halfhearted concessions to change and inclusion occurred, albeit always seeming to be too little too late. This organization (curiously, initiated by a retired British official) might have seemed impotent at first, but it did demand that "the Government should be widened and that the people should have their proper and legitimate share in it."8 Perhaps most significantly, the initial meeting, held in Bombay in 1885, involved about seventy-two delegates, from various regions, and consisted mostly of upper class Hindus and Parsis (many of them lawyers) with only two Muslims in attendance. It was through this organization, under the leadership of lawyers such as Motilal Nehru and his son Jawaharlal (India's first prime minister), and M. K. Gandhi, that India achieved independence.

Such a meeting, let alone the organization itself (or, for that matter, the nationalist/independence movement), would not have been possible had it not been for the English language as a lingua franca, which stemmed from the 1835 decision by the Governor-General to make English the official language of instruction. That decision opened a can of worms: men educated in English law saw the possibilities of constitutional democracy. No one Indian language could claim the majority of speakers, and English provided the bridge that made communication possible between the educated from different parts of India. The importance of this development cannot be overemphasized. Related developments included the establishment of universities (oddly, in 1857) in Bombay, Madras, and Calcutta; a vibrant (if often censored) press, and Indian literature in English. These all are evident and thriving yet today, and strongly so. The most important development might well have been that of nationalism, an attempt to override the British policy of divide-and-rule (which played on Hindu-Muslim antipathy). Of course, the creation of Pakistan showed that the dream was not completely successful—yet India today is a successful democracy. And the nationalist movement did bring the diverse cultures and languages, the religious sects and castes, into a new identity: Indian.

Conclusion

The date 1900 makes a good closing point. In 1899, Lord Curzon, the most imperial of the Viceroys, became Governor-General, and in 1901 the Queen-Empress, Victoria, died. The post-1857 developments were, of course, designed to keep empire supreme, but British tradition opened doors within the empire, and did so in spite of empire (e.g., the use of the Magna Carta by an Indian teacher in the classroom).9 Further, they really did not develop a coherent approach toward rule. The late Raghavan Iyer found it to be a mix of Trusteeship, Utilitarianism, Platonic Guardianship, and Evangelicalism.10 The focus was on administration, not development, and that by as small a cadre as possible. Stalin is said to have observed that it was ridiculous . . . that a few hundred Englishmen should dominate India. Actually, the "few hundred" numbered just over a thousand, of whom one-fifth were at any time either sick or on leave. This, over a population of about 300 million in what is now India, Pakistan, Myanmar, and Bangladesh.11 Although certainly not as cruel as the Belgians in the Congo, the servants of the Raj and their compatriots (families, businessmen, missionaries, etc.)— about 100,000 in 190012 —were viewed as "lofty and contemptuous."13 And they had their moments of cruelty as well.

The empire was a mix of the White Man's Burden and Ma-Bap ("We are your mother and father"). Mix is a good word to describe the Raj. The British engaged in racism and exploitation, and they also provided the doors that would lead to Indian democracy and nationhood. Paul Scott, in the opening to The Jewel in the Crown, the initial novel of the Raj Quartet, wrote of two nations in violent opposition

. . . locked in an imperial embrace of such long standing and subtlety it was no longer possible for them to know whether they hated or loved one another, or what it was that held them together and seemed to have confused the image of their separate destinies.14

CHAPTER III

Difference in the past and present life

Although there is a definite difference between past and present lifestyles, the difference between these two concepts may differ according to income, access to modern facilities, equipment, education, and lifestyle. There are some communities in the world who do not get access to many modern facilities and technological inventions. Therefore, the difference between past and present lifestyles can be a very subjective topic and the differences here might differ in various people's experience.

The key difference between past and present lifestyles is that the past lifestyle can be described as a simple, traditional, home-based lifestyle with a self-sufficient economy and simple tools. Present lifestyle, on the other hand, is complex, efficient, comfortable, and modern, highly technological, and is based on a profit maximizing production economy. The complexity or sophistication of the lifestyle may however depend on the income level, geographical location and culture.

We can compare and contrast the Past and Present Lifestyles under many different areas such as attitudes, feelings of people, and thinking capacity of people, food habits, clothes, housing, transport, use of tools and machinery, education system, economy, etc.

Difference Between Past and Present Lifestyles in terms of Attitudes, Feelings, and Thinking Capacity

Attitudes and Feelings:

Past: Attitudes of people in the past would have been more peaceful since they did not have any complex economic, social or political problems. Thus, their attitudes and feelings were much simple than the present day.

Present: People in the present are more educated, open and free to express their opinions. With the complexity of their new lifestyle, their attitudes and feelings have become more complex.

Thinking Capacity:

Past: Our ancestors were intelligent and had a great thinking capacity despite the lack of technology and tools such as calculators, computers, etc. The technology we used today is a result of their innovations. In addition, we still have not been able to figure out some of their work. Ex: constructions such as pyramids, ancient irrigation systems.

Present: The thinking capacity of people has widened. Even a person with limited thinking capacity has the ability to improve it with education, access to books, magazines, and the internet.

Modern technology may also have a negative influence on intelligence. For example, some people use the internet to look solutions for their question, without thinking critically.

Difference Between Past and Present Lifestyles in terms of Food Habits Changes in Food Habits:

Past: Before Stone Age, people used to eat fruits, leaves and anything they found from the forest. But, this habit changed into hunting animals, preserving food items and planting and growing vegetables, which eventually led into farming different crops like maize, corn, and rice. People were healthy, they rarely had diseases and never needed extra exercise cause their daily work kept their bodies running.

Present: At present, we have turned the agriculture into a mass scale production, including machinery, technology, pesticides and weedicides, all which came in with the green revolution. With green revolution agriculture and the traditional farming culture turned upside down. As for now, farmers who are able to cope up with the multi-national cooperation's and their large-scale, expensive products, pesticides and high-yielding varieties of seeds, keep producing crops for the market. Yet the traditional, low-income farmers even today, especially in Asian countries, are in a dire state.

Fast food is another major factor in modern food habits. Although many people find it convenient, it leads to many health conditions. Today people are unhealthy, needs medicine and functions on diets and exercise machines.

Past lifestyle was based on agriculture.

Difference Between Past and Present Lifestyles in terms of Economy

Past: With the Agriculture based economy, people bartered goods.

Present: We are today moving towards an industrial economy which is cooperating with the service sector; as a survival factor agriculture keeps these two sectors running in a successful way by giving the needed supply for their daily demand on food consumption.

Difference Between Past and Present Lifestyles and Clothing

Past: In the past, people used to wear simple clothes made out of dry leaves; later, they slowly moved into different types of clothing. With the industrial revolution, this situation changed. People who had to work in industries had to cover themselves up in order to make sure they didn't get exposed to the chemicals or any other harmful things. Therefore, long dresses, full body covered clothes came into the society. Later clothing changed in terms of the place you lived, your culture, ethnicity, and religion. For example, Indians used to cover themselves up with salwar, sarees, etc. whereas the western Europe people tend to cover themselves up according to the climate; shorts in warm areas and jeans in cold regions.

Present: Aspects like comfort, trend, and style are what matters in clothing rather than the climate or region you live in. For example, Indians wear their traditional clothes on occasions, but they are more into western fashions like jeans, shorts, blouses, and T-shirts.

Difference Between Past and Present Lifestyles in terms of Education

Past: In terms of education in the past, people rarely got the chance to educate themselves. Farmers made sure that their children knew how to plot a farm and carry out their daily work. Yet with time, people went to the religious institutes like church, temple, kovil and mosque in order to learn. Later with the industrial revolution and factories and equipment coming into action, even the children of the agricultural families were sent to the town to learn how to work with machinery. Then later with colonization, people started learning languages and sciences with the improvement in knowledge. The most important fact is that all these changes in education happened only in the lives of the males as the females were kept at home to do the daily work like sweeping, sewing, painting, embroidery, cleaning and looking after children.

Present: With the revolutions and freedom actions taking place all over the world, females started to fight for their rights in terms of voting, education, and politics. These freedom fights were granted after several struggles. Today, women have the opportunity to get a good education despite their religion, ethnicity, and race .

People now have access to books, magazines, and the internet and students are much advanced in terms of education and access to knowledge. However, as mentioned in the beginning, there are exceptions to these facilities.

Difference Between Past and Present Lifestyles in Using Equipment and Machinery

Past: In the past, our ancestors used to work with small tools that were made out of animal bones or wood. Animals were also used for ploughing, carrying loads, etc.

Present: With evolution, people started to use metals to make equipment like knives, and other tools. Now, equipment are made out of several material such as carbon, fiber, and especially plastic to make things used for daily usage.

Today we use machines to do the same things with less effort and time. Machinery has made life easier on earth in terms of efficiency. However, weapons can be termed as a negative outcome of the equipment evolution.

Difference Between Past and Present Lifestyles in terms of Transport Animals vs Vehicles

Past: In the past, people used animals like horses, donkeys, and camels to travel from one place to another.

Present: With advancement in technology, transportation has become much wider, easier, and faster; there are a variety of vehicles to travel on land, air, and water.

When talking about transportation on water, during ancient times, travels by ships took a long time, and many people died because of the weather and bad conditions of the ships. But today, there are luxury cruisers that carry supermarkets, tennis courts, swimming pools, houses, etc. Many people use airplanes to travel between countries.

Difference Between Past and Present Lifestyles in terms of Housing

Past: In the past, people lived in caves, mud, and wood huts, etc. They used natural ingredients to build their houses.

Present: Housing over the past few decades have changed in terms of shape, mode of creation, size, place and purpose and so on. Today material such as bricks, cement, plastic and anything and everything is used in housing. Technology advancement has given freedom for the human being to go beyond nature to create human dwellings.

Difference Between Past and Present Lifestyles in terms of Religion and Beliefs

Past: During the past, people lived with the concepts of religion, nature, economy and village. These concepts were always bound to one another. Religion dictated their whole lives.

Present: But today the situation has changed. People are too busy to pay any attention to their religion and beliefs. The advancement of science and technology has also led people to question the validity of religion.

CHAPTER IV

Live with the present as INDIA does

After all this bullsh*t you read about the british's fake impact on INDIA hers what we the Indians and the whole INDIA together are at with the world. The below is an extrct from LONDON School of economics saying why INDIA is the next superpower.

According to the 'World Population Review 2021,' the powerful country in the world is the United States, followed by China, Russia, Germany, and the United Kingdom.

The survey ranks 80 countries on the basis of five criteria: international and military alliances, political and economic influence, and leadership skills.

Also read | Make India the world's biggest military power: PM inaugurates 7 defence firms

The US tops the list with a massive GDP of $21 trillion. Meanwhile, China has a GDP of $14 trillion.

Despite being defended by US Biden Joe Biden as a 'necessary measure,' the controversial withdrawal of troops from Afghanistan after two decades of war, the country is being deemed as a hegemon in retreat by critics.

Also read | Live firings & high levels of exercises introduced in Malabar: Karambir Singh

President Vladimir Putin had himself said that the US and Russia no longer decide the answers to the most important questions in the world.

He added that China and Germany are headed for superpower status due to the waning influence and the US.

India occupies the 13th spot on the list with a GDP of almost $3 trillion. Its rich talent pool and affordable connectivity are crucial factors that will improve its ranking in the future.

Also see | In Pics: All the countries with which China is in a territorial dispute

Amid the evolving Asian balance of power, India's strength lies in its strategic location.

As a result, countries such as the US, Japan, and Australia are working closely with India to combat China's growing influence in the Indo-Pacific region.

From 1991 to 2019, India's GDP by Purchasing Power Parity (PPP) has increased by 772 per cent from $1 trillion to $9 trillion.

However, the country's population has grown 209 per cent from 1960 to 2021, that is, from 450 million to 1.39 billion people.

While this reduces the per capita income, in the long term, this growth will keep the country's labour force young and large.

This will provide India a major economic advantage over the US, China, and the European Union, which will face a decline in there labour force in the next 30 years.

India's PPP is expected to reach $43 trillion and surpass the US by 2050 making it the second-largest economy in the world after China.

To boost its infrastructure, India is focusing on several large-scale megaprojects to develop a golden quadrilateral between its metropolitan cities.

In addition to its 11 corridor projects, it is concentrating on a $75 billion national highways and roadways programme called 'Bharatmala' and 'Sagarmala' project worth $116 million to build new mega ports and establish 14 coastal economic zones.

India has allocated its defence spending budget 2.5 per cent of its GDP in the last three decades. Because of this, the country's defence budget along with its economy are skyrocketing.

In 2019, India had spent $71 billion on its military, which is almost double its budget a decade ago.

It has the third-largest defence budget in the world behind the US and China.

From a booming high-tech sector to elite educational institutes, India has the potential to become a superpower with rapid digitalisation.

Although the increased competition leads to faster economic growth and technological innovation, most economies are not prone to accept change easily.

Armed conflict is often the result of the rapid rise and military and economic power. It is a major challenge to harness the spirit of challenge while avoiding its ripple effect.

I conclude it all that we should adapt ourselves to the changes an live with the present without even giving a f**ck to the past.

By the way, the example of INDIA and the British gives us an idea and rememberence how great we Indians are and of an slogan:

"BAAP TO BAAP HOTA HAI" (Hindi)

Dad is just not dad but he is the god that can easily overcome the sons of the bit*ches(British)